Pumpkin Patch

Scare up some bewitchin' fun!
Celebrate the most fun night of the year with glowing Jack-o-Lanterns and bountiful pumpkins.

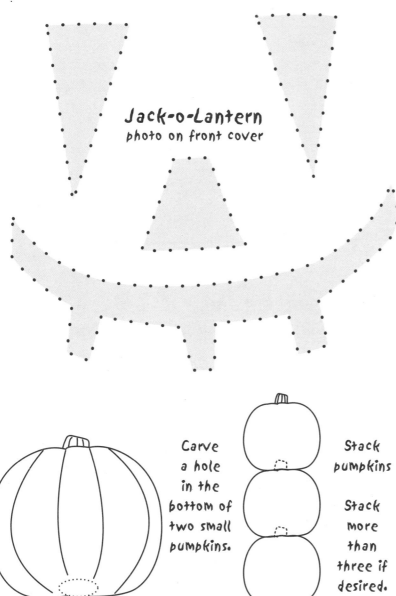

Jack-o-Lantern
photo on front cover

Carve a hole in the bottom of two small pumpkins.

Stack pumpkins

Stack more than three if desired.

For a color catalog featuring over 200 terrific 'How-To' books,
visit www.d-originals.com

Size the Pattern
Enlarge or reduce the pattern on a copy machine or computer to fit your pumpkin.

Prepare Pattern
Trace or photocopy the pattern. Trim pattern, leaving a 1/2" border around the design. Tape the pattern as flat against the pumpkin as possible (make small cuts or tucks as needed).

Transfer Pattern
Poke dots into the pumpkin (see patterns). If the design is hard to see, connect dots with a dull lead pencil. Or rub flour over the dots to make them easier to see.

Work Slowly
Go slowly and take your time.

Carve the Pumpkin
• Hold the pumpkin in your lap.
• Saw steadily with a continuous up-and-down motion.
• Keep gentle pressure.
• Saw dot-to-dot.
• Remove and reinsert the saw to make corners. Push cut pieces out with a finger, not the saw.
• Carve small areas first.

Carve from the Inside
Carve from the inside of the design to the outside.

Angle the Edges
Carve edges at an angle for smooth lines & better illumination. Carve the flattest side of pumpkin.

Don't Use Candles
Keep plastic pumpkins away from all lit flames. Do not use a candle to light a plastic pumpkin. Use only battery powered lights.

Tips for Carving Real Pumpkins

Select Pumpkins
Pick a firm, unblemished pumpkin with smooth skin.

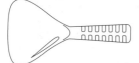

Clean and Scrape
Scoop out seeds and strings with a pumpkin scoop or flat-edge ice cream scoop. Scrape inner pulp away from the area you plan to carve until the pumpkin wall is approximately 1" thick.

Slow Dehydration
Pumpkins last longer when you keep them cool. Keep them dry to prevent mold.

Coat Surfaces
Coating all cut surfaces, including the inside, with petroleum jelly seals in the pumpkin's moisture.

Pumpkin Fresh
There is also an easy to apply spray-on, environmentally friendly preserver called Pumpkin Fresh! that contains all natural ingredients and works well to deter bugs, rot, and mold.

Cut the Bottom
Tip: Cut off the bottom rather than the top of the pumpkin. This allows you to position a carved pumpkin over a light instead of reaching in through the top to turn on your Jack O Lantern.

Battery Lights
Use battery powered lights (instead of candles) in pumpkins for a fire-safe Halloween.

All Smiles
photo on front cover

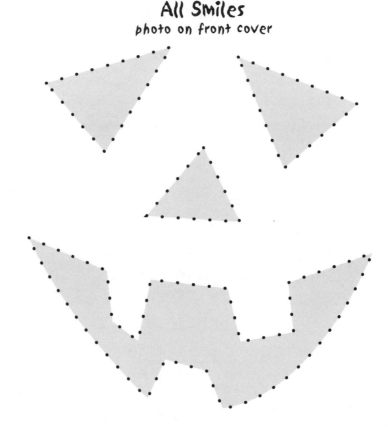

As the pumpkin sheds its light, witches will wave their magic wands o'er you tonight.

Bad Hair Day
photo on front cover

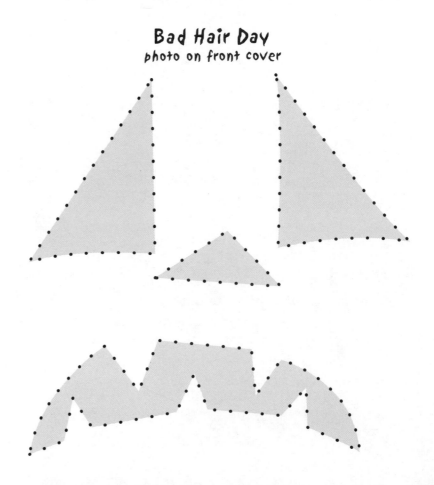

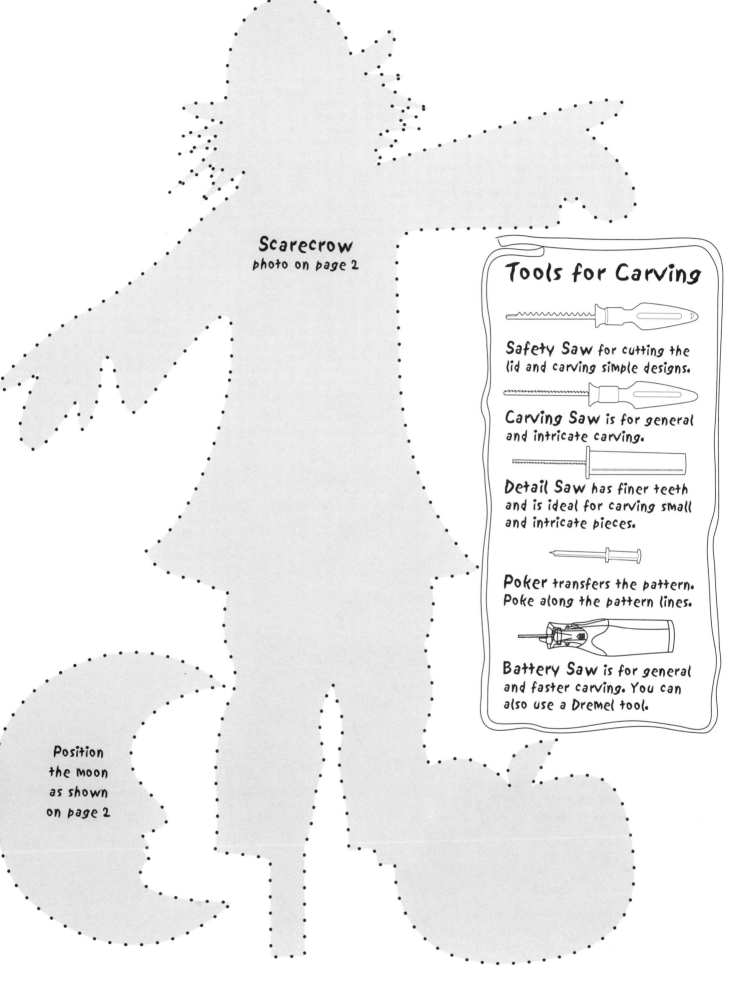

Scarecrow
photo on page 2

Position
the moon
as shown
on page 2

Tools for Carving

Safety Saw for cutting the lid and carving simple designs.

Carving Saw is for general and intricate carving.

Detail Saw has finer teeth and is ideal for carving small and intricate pieces.

Poker transfers the pattern. Poke along the pattern lines.

Battery Saw is for general and faster carving. You can also use a Dremel tool.

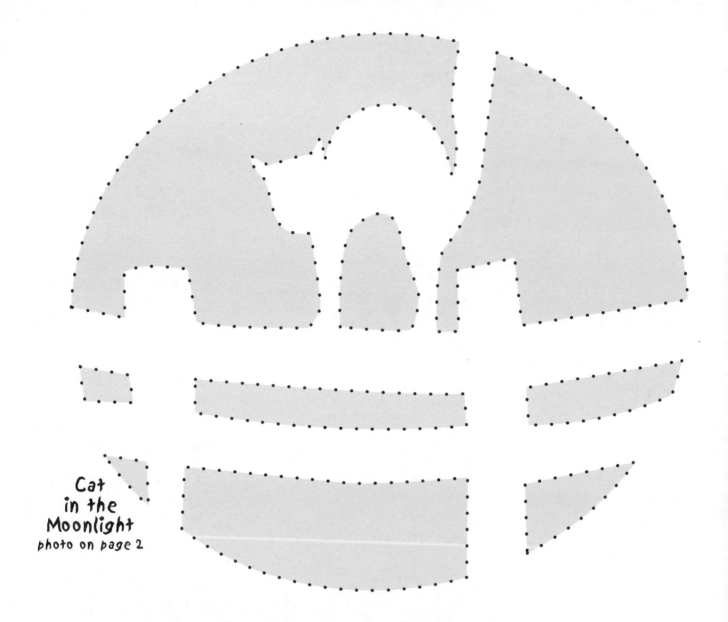

Cat
in the
Moonlight
photo on page 2

**When black cats prowl
and pumpkins gleam
May luck be yours
on Halloween.**

How to Incise
Designs on a Pumpkin

Scratch through the surface skin of
your pumpkin to "incise" designs such as
the "Xs" on this pumpkin face.

Frankenstein
photo on page 2

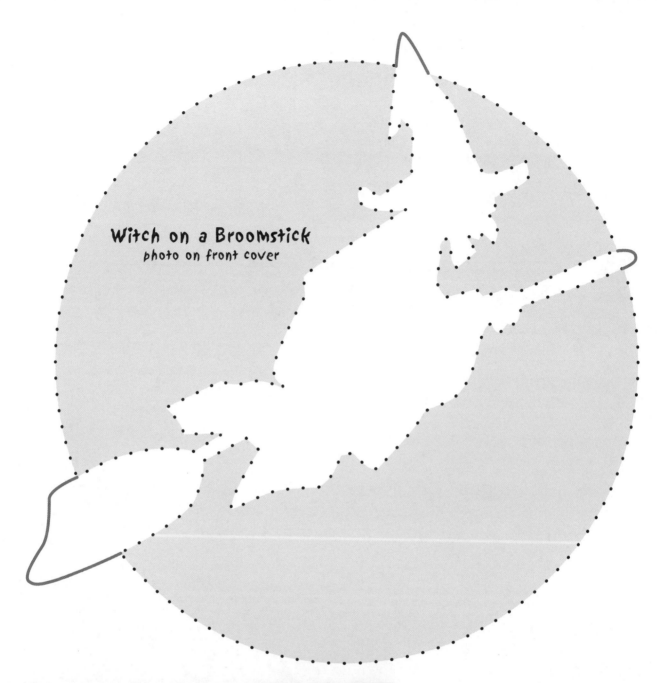

Witch on a Broomstick
photo on front cover

"Out for mischief – Halloween"

May all the Witches that here are seen Bring you good luck on Halloween.

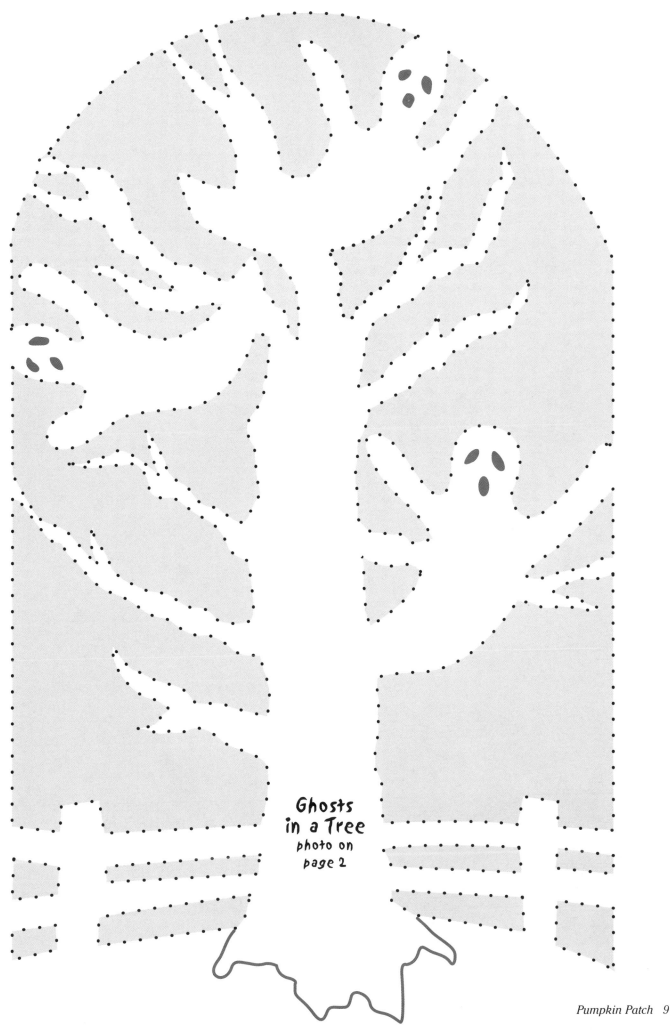

Ghosts
in a Tree
photo on
page 2

Spider in the Window
photo on front cover

HISS! and HARK!
Draw close and tremble.
'Tis this night
that ghosts assemble!

Scary Face
photo on back cover

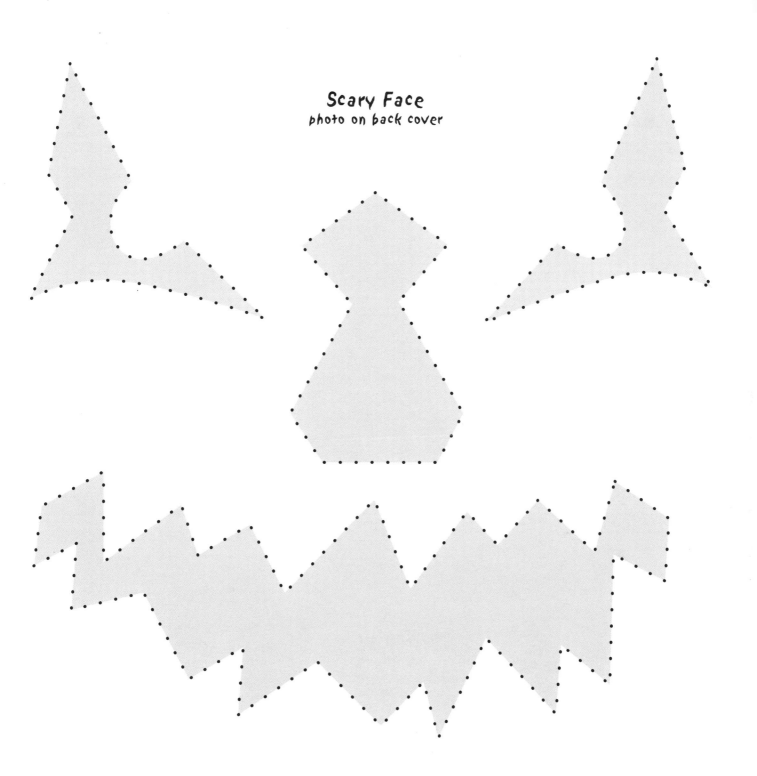

Spooks and witches are busy tonight,
Anxious to put good children to fright;
Let's get together to ward off the charm,
Laugh and be merry, and forget all alarm.

WITCH

WAY

Witch Way
photo on
back cover

Carve the
pumpkin then
add the words
with Black
felt alphabet
stickers.

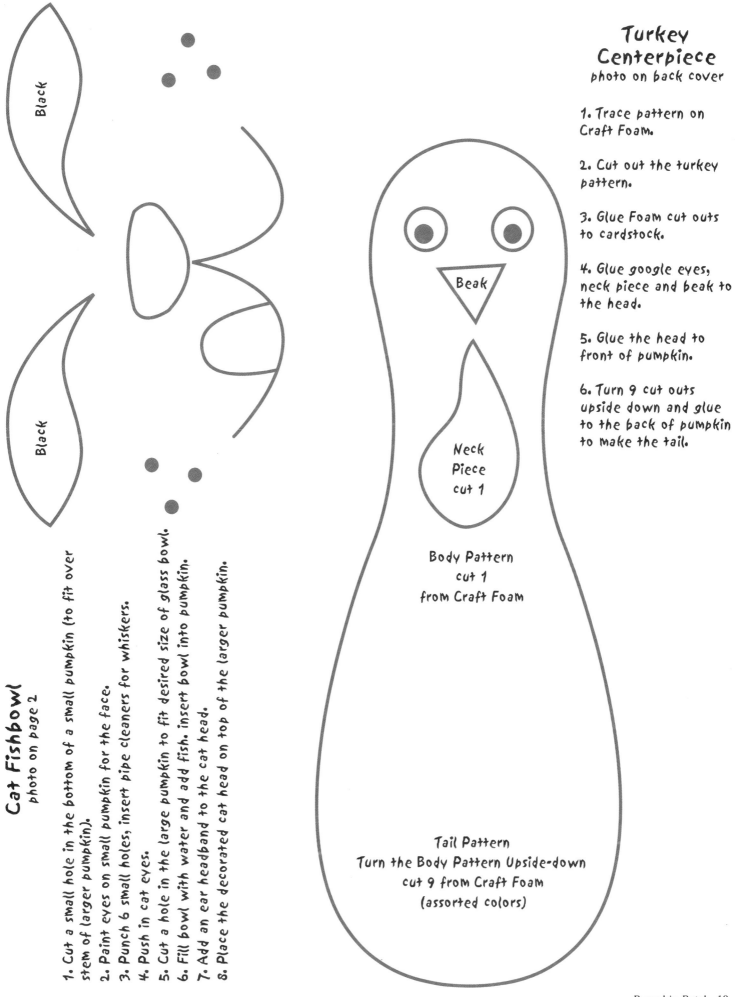

1. Trace pattern on Craft Foam.

2. Cut out the turkey pattern.

3. Glue Foam cut outs to cardstock.

4. Glue google eyes, neck piece and beak to the head.

5. Glue the head to front of pumpkin.

6. Turn 9 cut outs upside down and glue to the back of pumpkin to make the tail.

Black

Black

Beak

Neck
Piece
cut 1

Body Pattern
cut 1
from Craft Foam

Tail Pattern
Turn the Body Pattern Upside-down
cut 9 from Craft Foam
(assorted colors)

Cat Fishbowl
photo on page 2

1. Cut a small hole in the bottom of a small pumpkin (to fit over stem of larger pumpkin).

2. Paint eyes on small pumpkin for the face.

3. Punch 6 small holes, insert pipe cleaners for whiskers.

4. Push in cat eyes.

5. Cut a hole in the large pumpkin to fit desired size of glass bowl.

6. Fill bowl with water and add fish. insert bowl into pumpkin.

7. Add an ear headband to the cat head.

8. Place the decorated cat head on top of the larger pumpkin.

Bat

photo on page 27

1. Trace bat pattern onto Black craft foam and cut out.

2. Lightly score along fold lines. Fold as shown in diagram.

3. Cut ears and score along fold lines. Glue ear upright. Glue on eyes.

4. Tie a raffia bow and glue it to the stem. Glue the Black bat on top of the bow.

Craft Foam can be cut with scissors. It will hold a fold if scored. To score, place a staight edge along the fold line. Draw a ballpoint pen along the straight edge. Do not press too hard or the pen will cut through the foam. Fold away from the scored line.

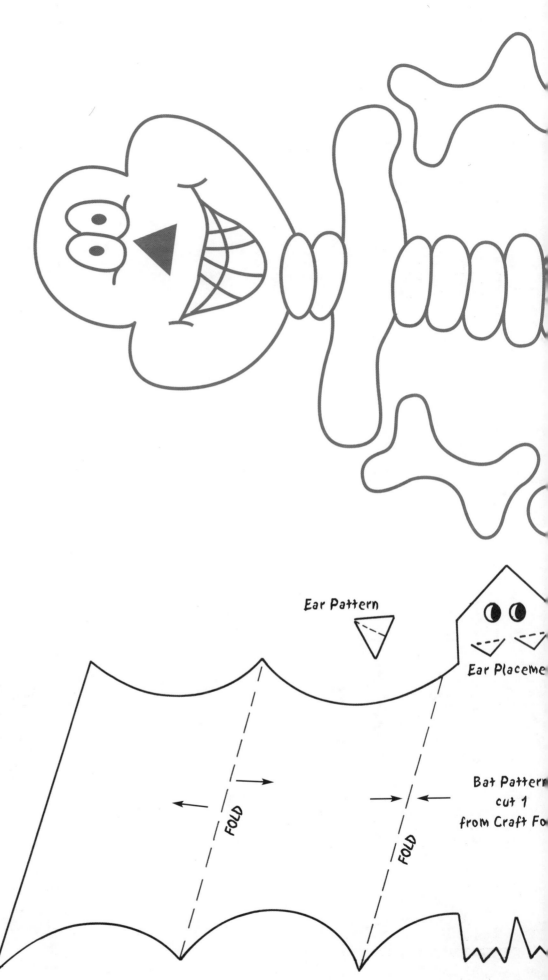

Ear Pattern

Ear Placeme[nt]

Bat Pattern
cut 1
from Craft Fo[am]

FOLD

FOLD

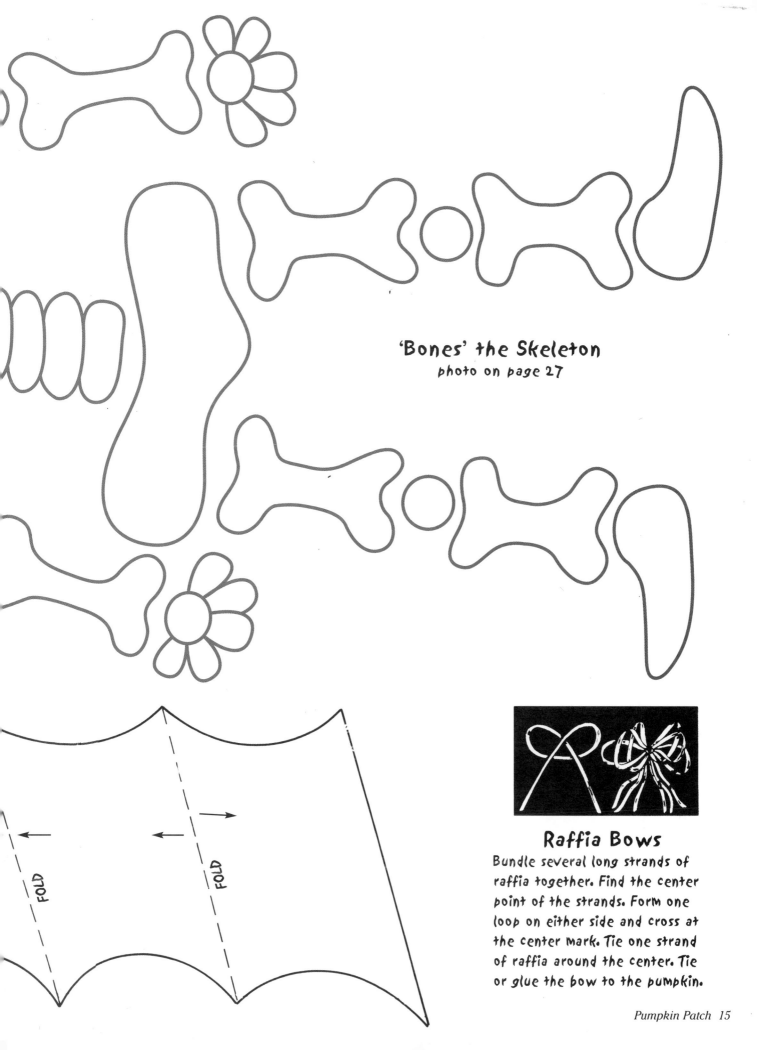

'Bones' the Skeleton
photo on page 27

FOLD

FOLD

Raffia Bows

Bundle several long strands of raffia together. Find the center point of the strands. Form one loop on either side and cross at the center mark. Tie one strand of raffia around the center. Tie or glue the bow to the pumpkin.

Yellow

Yellow

Scarecrow
photo on page 27

1. Place one crate on its side. Insert into overalls. Push crate down as far as it will go. Place a second crate on top of first. Button shirt around the second crate, sliding shirt collar forward toward the edge of crate. Pull overall bib up over shirt. Tuck in shirt tails and buckle straps over the top of second crate.

2. Stuff shirt sleeves with newspaper. Stuff gloves with small pieces of newspaper. Tuck gloves and short pieces of raffia into shirt cuffs. Glue or sew gloves to cuffs.

3. With scarecrow in sitting position, stuff legs with newspaper. Stuff boots and slide into legs. Arrange short pieces of raffia around boots. Tie 18" of jute tightly around each pant leg, raffia and boot. Repeat for other leg.

4. Cut some raffia to 30". Bundle pieces together and tie in the center. Glue center of rafia bundle to top of pumpkin. Spread out to form hair. Cut, bend and glue straw hat over hair.

5. Set body on a chair, box, or hay bale. Arrange arms and legs. Set pumpkin head on top of body to complete the scarecrow.

Yellow

Painted 'Black Cat'
photo on page 27

Don't scat a black cat on Halloween night
and all that you wish for will surely come right.

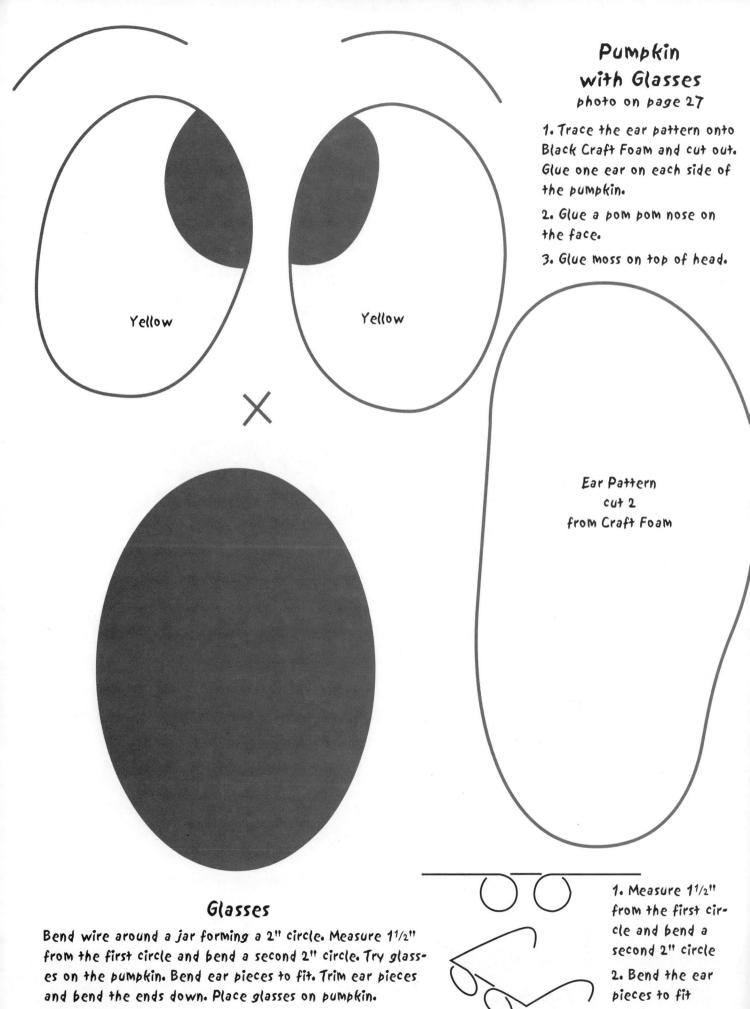

Pumpkin with Glasses
photo on page 27

1. Trace the ear pattern onto Black Craft Foam and cut out. Glue one ear on each side of the pumpkin.

2. Glue a pom pom nose on the face.

3. Glue moss on top of head.

Yellow

Yellow

Ear Pattern
cut 2
from Craft Foam

Glasses

Bend wire around a jar forming a 2" circle. Measure 1½" from the first circle and bend a second 2" circle. Try glasses on the pumpkin. Bend ear pieces to fit. Trim ear pieces and bend the ends down. Place glasses on pumpkin.

1. Measure 1½" from the first circle and bend a second 2" circle

2. Bend the ear pieces to fit

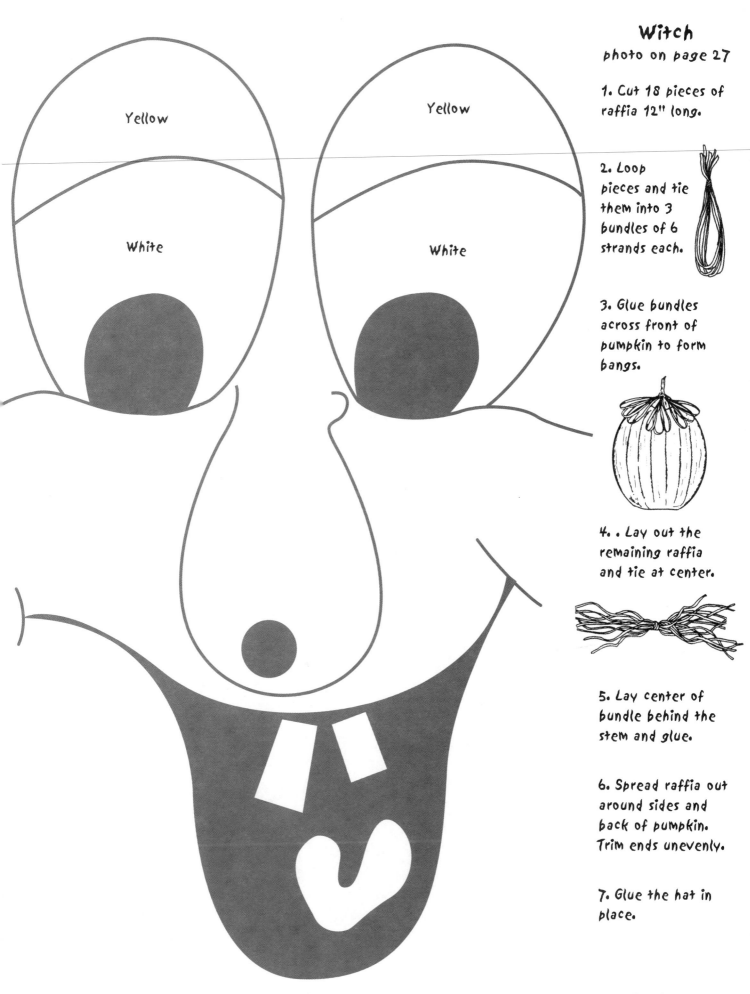

Yellow

Yellow

White

White

1. Cut 18 pieces of raffia 12" long.

2. Loop pieces and tie them into 3 bundles of 6 strands each.

3. Glue bundles across front of pumpkin to form bangs.

4. . Lay out the remaining raffia and tie at center.

5. Lay center of bundle behind the stem and glue.

6. Spread raffia out around sides and back of pumpkin. Trim ends unevenly.

7. Glue the hat in place.

Yellow

Yellow

Clown
photo on page 27

Neck Ruffle

Cut two 9" x 45" strips of fabric. Sew or glue the ends to form a circle.

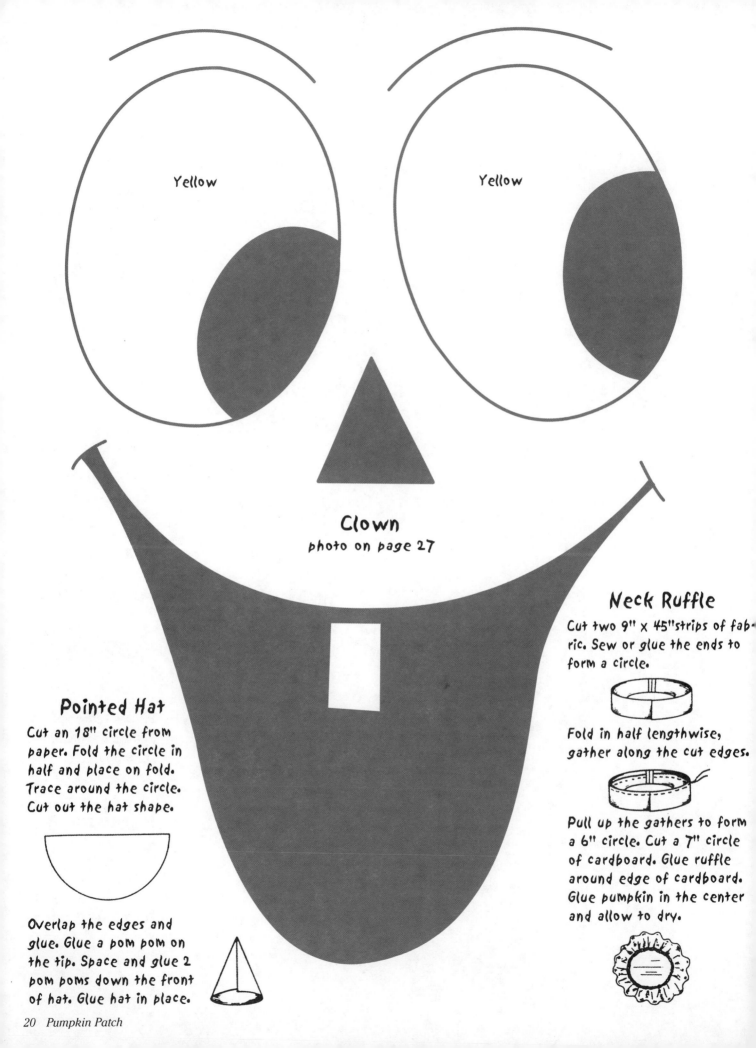

Fold in half lengthwise, gather along the cut edges.

Pull up the gathers to form a 6" circle. Cut a 7" circle of cardboard. Glue ruffle around edge of cardboard. Glue pumpkin in the center and allow to dry.

Pointed Hat

Cut an 18" circle from paper. Fold the circle in half and place on fold. Trace around the circle. Cut out the hat shape.

Overlap the edges and glue. Glue a pom pom on the tip. Space and glue 2 pom poms down the front of hat. Glue hat in place.

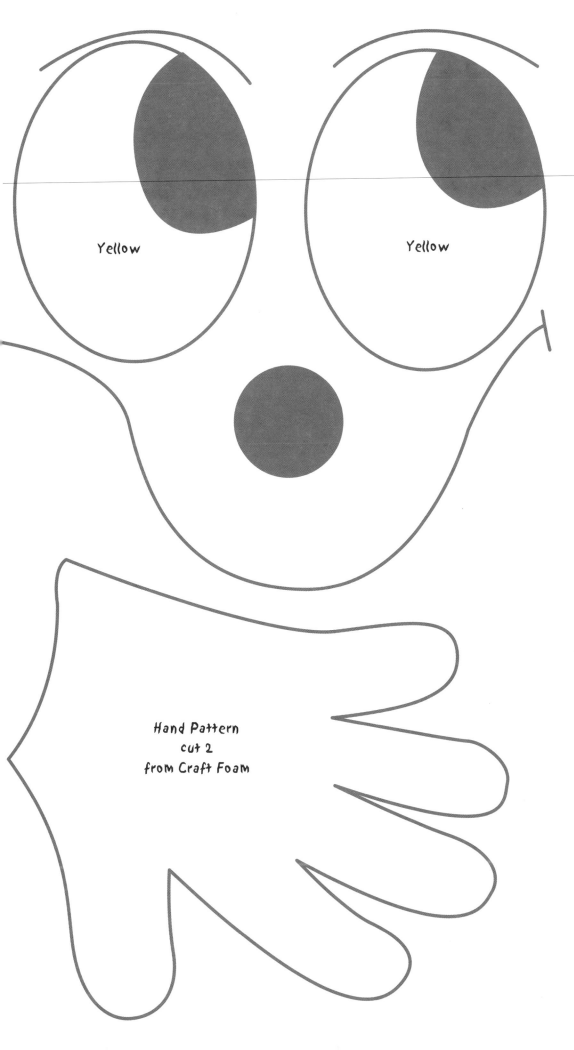

Yellow   Yellow

Hand Pattern
cut 2
from Craft Foam

Pumpkin with Tennis Shoes
photo on page 27

1. Cut out the backs of small tennis shoes.

2. Tie the laces in the bottom 2 holes of each shoe. Apply glue to soles and place pumpkin on top of shoes.

3. Trace the hand pattern onto Black Craft Foam and cut out.

4. Glue the hands, with thumbs up, to the sides of pumpkin.

Yellow   Yellow

Spider Sitting on a Pumpkin
photo on back cover

1. Place 4 chenille stems side by side. Find the center of all stems. Group all 4 stems and twist them together at the center. Spread legs out into a circle.

2. Bend 1/2" up at the end of each leg to make the feet.

3. Measure up from ea foot and bend dowr form legs.

4. Glue a pom over center of legs.

5. Glue wi gle eyes t pom pom.

6. Glue spi to pumpkin

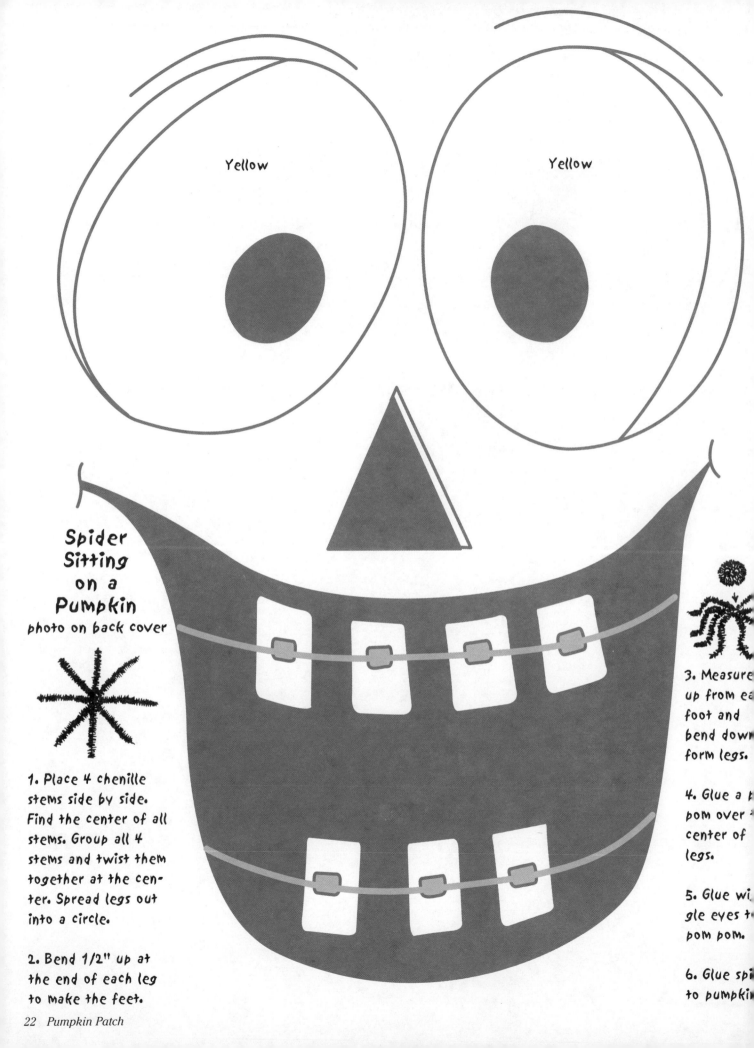

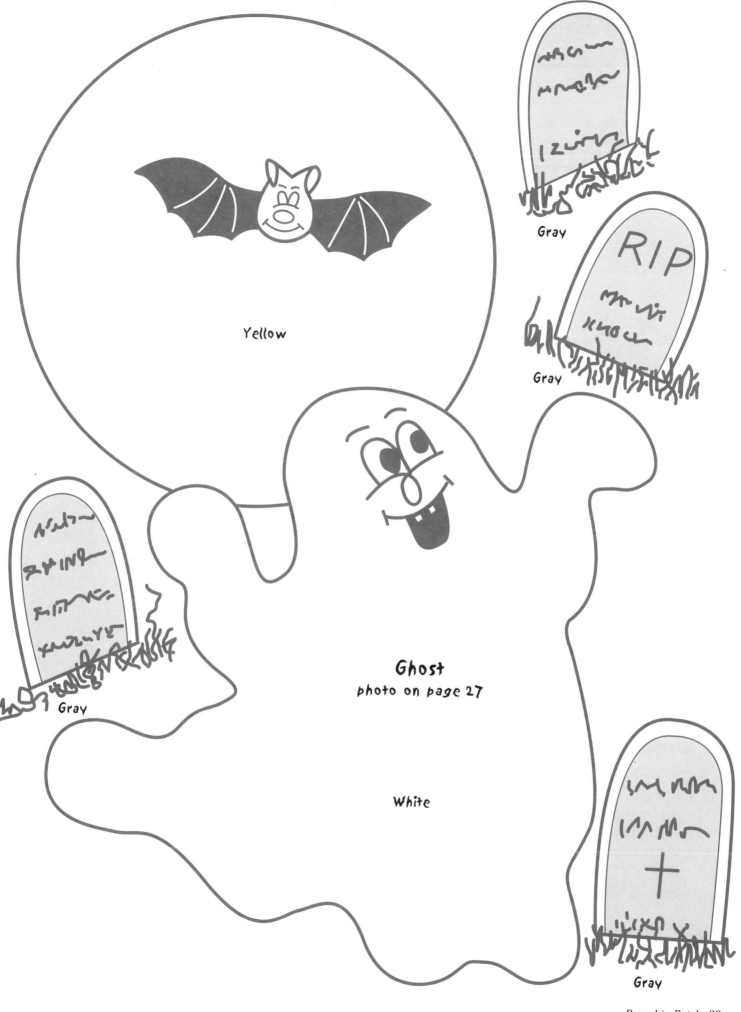

Yellow

Gray

RIP

Gray

Ghost
photo on page 27

White

Gray

Gray

Pumpkin with Fall Flowers
photo on front cover

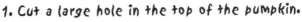

1. Cut a large hole in the top of the pumpkin.
2. Paint the face.
3. Use the pumpkin as a vase for silk flowers.
4. Or insert a glass bowl filled with water to hold an arrangement of fresh flowers

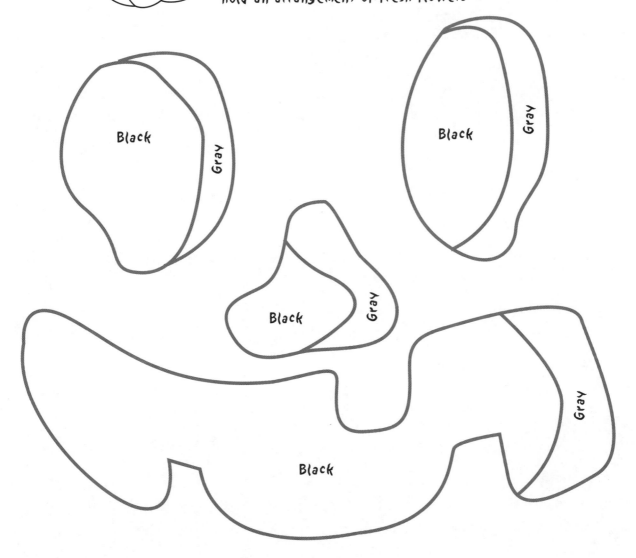

Black
Gray

Black
Gray

Black
Gray

Black

Gray

Paper Sack Pumpkins
Purchase Orange gift bags or lunch sacks, or paint a brown paper bag with Orange spray paint.

Transfer a pattern.

Paint the design.

Let it dry.

Stuff with wadded newspaper.

Tie the top of sack with raffia to close it.

*When your fortune
you are told,
Do not think me overbold
To hope that I will be the one
Your true love when
the year is done.*

Mummy
photo on page 27

A quick trick for coloring a
pumpkin is to use a large
permanent black marker.
Simply go over the lines
and fill in the spaces!

Tips for Painting Pumpkins

Pick a Pumpkin
For best decorating results, pick a firm, unblemished pumpkin with smooth skin.

Size the Pattern
Enlarge or reduce the pattern on a copy machine or computer to fit your pumpkin.

Transfer Pattern
Trace the pattern onto tracing paper or copy it. Place graphite paper under the traced pattern. Tape to pumpkin. Lightly trace the face with a ballpoint pen. Lift a corner of the pattern to be sure the lines have transferred.

Use Acrylic Paint
Use acrylic paint (Black, White, Yellow, Pink) to create faces. Refer to color photos for color placement.

Paintbrushes
Use flat brushes to paint the solid areas. Use a liner brush for small details.

Finish the Pumpkin
Allow the paint to dry completely. Spray the entire pumpkin with a clear acrylic coating.

Glue
Use hot glue to attach embellishments. Use caution with hot glue.

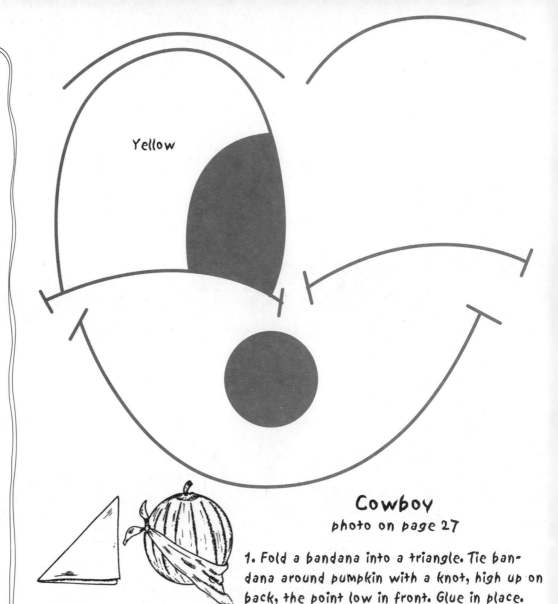

Yellow

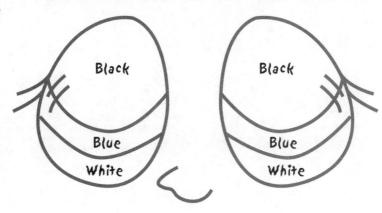

Cowboy
photo on page 27

1. Fold a bandana into a triangle. Tie bandana around pumpkin with a knot, high up on back, the point low in front. Glue in place.

2. Coil 3 loops of jute and tie with a single knot. Glue to left side of bandana. Drape the tail of the jute cord across the front and glue to the right side of the bandana.

3. Place a hat on the side of head and glue in place.

Black   Black

Blue   Blue
White   White

Baby Face
photo on page 27 and on back cover

Cut a hole for the mouth.

Insert a baby's pacifier.

TIP: This pumpkin is perfect for a baby shower centerpiece.